STARK

LEKTÜRE ENGLISCH

Alan Cartmell

The Green Feather

für die Unterstufe

STARK

Umschlagbild: Rainer Thiele

ISBN: 3-89449-446-8

Inhalt

Autor: Alan Cartmell
Illustrator: Rainer Thiele

Vorwort

Liebe Schülerinnen, liebe Schüler,

Amanda darf ihre Sommerferien bei ihrer Kousine Brenda und ihrem Kousin Peter auf dem Land verbringen. Auf der Zugfahrt dorthin lernt sie einen seltsamen Jungen namens Arthur kennen, der nach einem kurzem Gespräch plötzlich verschwindet und nur eine wunderschöne goldgrüne Feder hinterlässt. Amandas Neugierde ist geweckt und als sie, Brenda und Peter auch noch eine alte Holztruhe auf dem Dachboden finden, in die eine ähnliche Feder geschnitzt ist, ist sie entschlossen, mehr über den mysteriösen Arthur herauszufinden. Was sie dabei erfährt und was es mit der grünen Feder auf sich hat, kannst du in dieser Geschichte nachlesen.
Schwierige Wörter sind auf Deutsch erklärt, damit euch das Lesen leichter fällt.

Ich wünsche euch viel Spaß bei eurer Lektüre!

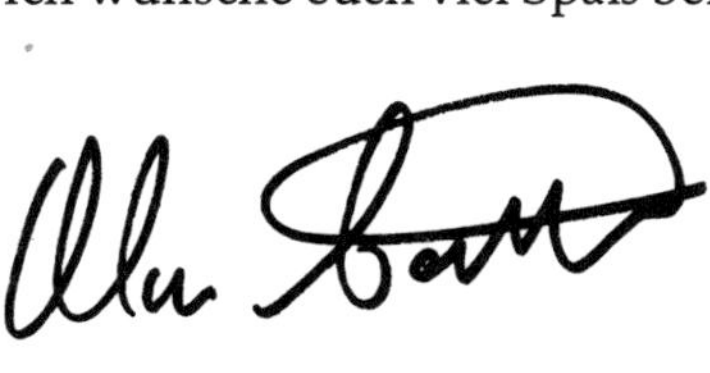

Alan Cartmell

Chapter 1
Amanda meets a strange boy

"Come on, Amanda," called Mrs James, her mother, "your father is waiting in the car." Amanda finished tying up[1] her long fair hair with a hair band and took one last look in the mirror. Then she picked up her suitcase and rucksack and rushed down the stairs.

"Goodbye Mum," she said, kissing her on the cheek.

"Give my love to Aunty Rachel, Uncle Bob, Brenda and Peter," called Mum, as Amanda ran to the car.

"You're an old slow-coach[2]," said her father. "Quick. Fasten your seat belt. The train leaves Basington station in twenty minutes! I hope you've got your ticket."

***

Amanda waved to her mother as they drove down the road and then sat back and watched the old familiar places in the village go past: the sweet shop and post office where Mr Assan, the owner, always wore his turban, the pub called the Baker's Arms where Dad sometimes went for a beer, the farm with the animals which she sometimes visited, and over the little bridge

---

1 *to tie up* – festbinden
2 *slow-coach* – Trödelsuse

where her brother Sam once fell in the stream[3]. Amanda smiled as she remembered Sam coming home "like a drowned rat" as her father said. Then finally, as they went past the school, she thought: "No more English or maths for four whole weeks." She loved telling stories, but writing them down was always difficult. She always got a "C" for her English homework. "I've heard you telling your friends lovely stories, Amanda," said her teacher Mrs Hemming, "if you could only write them down you would get an "A"."

When they arrived at Basington Station the train was just coming in to the platform. Amanda got on the train and Father called out, as the train started to move: "Give my love to everybody."

***

Amanda found a seat, put her suitcase and rucksack on the luggage rack[4], and started to look at the book she had brought with her. The book was called "Dancing tonight" and was about the exciting adventures of Joy, a young ballet dancer. Amanda had just reached the part where Joy was dancing her first solo part, when a voice said: "Tickets, please." And the ticket collector came into the compartment. Oh dear! Where was her ticket? She had been so interested in Joy's adventures, she had forgotten about her ticket. She quickly took her ruck-

3 *stream* – Bächlein
4 *luggage rack* – Gepäckablage

sack from the luggage rack and opened it. In it were presents for Aunty Rachel and Uncle Bob, presents for her cousins Brenda and Peter, some sandwiches for lunch on the train and some clean handkerchiefs.

"Tickets, please." The ticket collector was already at the seat behind her. Then she remembered. The pocket with the zip[5] on the outside of the rucksack. Yes, there was the ticket. "Thank you, miss," said the guard as he clipped it. "Have a nice journey."

Amanda put her things back in the rucksack and sat back with a sigh of relief[6].

The train was going quite fast now and she put down her book to look out of the window and watch the fields of yellow corn and meadows with cows go quickly past; sometimes she saw brown rabbits.

While she was watching, she thought of her cousin Brenda's house. She hoped that, like last year, they would have fun exploring the fields and woods around it.

---

5 *zip* – Reißverschluss
6 *sigh of relief* – Seufzer der Erleichterung

"Now you are ten you can go on your own," her father had said at the start of the summer holidays. Amanda could still hear the "whoopee" her cousins Brenda and Peter had shouted when she had told Aunty Rachel on the phone. Brenda and Peter were twins and ten, too. She was also looking forward to[7] seeing Blackie. Blackie was the horse that Brenda told her she was learning to ride.

***

When Amanda had finished daydreaming and staring out of the window, she looked across at the seat opposite.

7 *to look forward to* – sich freuen auf

There was a young boy about her own age sitting in it. She hadn't seen him sit down and he was dressed a little strangely. He was wearing old rough brown woollen clothes and on his head he had a hat made of leather[8]. In it was a long green feather. He was smiling at her.

"Hello, Amanda," he said, "are you looking forward to going to the house on the hill again?"

"Who are you?" asked Amanda. "How do you know my name?"

"My name is Arthur," he replied. "I saw you last year when you were playing in the woods near the big house on the hill. I heard you telling Brenda those wonderful stories. Do you remember?"

"I don't remember seeing you," said Amanda rather rudely[9].

She thought back to last year and, yes, she had made up stories. They had been lying on their backs under the old oak tree in the clearing[10] in the woods. Aunty Rachel had said the tree was a thousand years old.

***

"Don't you remember the story of the boy and his old grandmother who lived in a cottage in the woods?"

---

8 *leather* – Leder
9 *rudely* – barsch
10 *clearing* – Lichtung

said Arthur. Amanda thought carefully. Yes, she did remember a story like that.

"But I don't think I told Brenda," she said. "How do you know it?" She had been looking out of the window as she puzzled over what the strange boy had said. When she looked back again there was nobody sitting in the seat.

"Where has he gone?" she wondered. "Oh, it's lunch time now, perhaps he went to the buffet car[11] for a drink or ice-cream. Funny he didn't say goodbye."

She took her sandwiches from her rucksack and decided she would like a drink, too. She went to the refreshment car and bought a cola. While[12] she was there she looked around for Arthur.

"I must see him in those funny old clothes," she thought to herself. She paid for her drink, looked again, but still couldn't see him.

She went back to her seat with her drink. Arthur still hadn't come back.

***

"Perhaps his parents are in another compartment[13]," she thought, "and won't let him go wandering about again." She felt very grown up being allowed to travel on her own.

---

11 *buffet car* – Speisewagen
12 *while* – während
13 *compartment* – Abteil

As she got to her seat, she glanced[14] at where Arthur had been sitting. There on the seat was a long green feather.

"He must have lost it from his hat," she thought.

She picked it up and looked at it. It was a beautiful feather. When she turned it in the light, the green turned to[15] gold and then back to green. She ran the feather along the back of her hand and felt it tingle[16]. And suddenly the story of the cottage in the forest came back into her mind. She put the feather down quickly on the table.

"It's a beautiful feather; I hope he comes back for it," she thought.

After she had finished her cola and sandwiches, she started reading again the exciting story of Joy, the ballet dancer. She was just on the last page when a voice came over the loud-speaker: "Five minutes to the next stop, Glenchurch. Glenchurch in five minutes."

Amanda quickly finished the book, put it in her rucksack and zipped it up. Soon she would be seeing her aunt and uncle and her cousins Brenda and Peter again.

***

---

14 *to glance* – starren
15 *to turn – hier:* wechseln
16 *to tingle* – prickeln

The train began to slow down and the platform slowly came into view. And there, waiting on the platform, were Brenda and Peter with Susie the black and white fox terrier. As Amanda took her suitcase from the luggage rack, she glanced at the table. The feather gleamed greeny-gold in the sunshine. Amanda picked it up quickly, tucked it under a strap of her rucksack and went to the door of the train.

Brenda and Peter, with Susie barking at their feet, helped her down from the train and took her over to the car where Uncle Bob was waiting. "I hope you had a good journey, Amanda," he said, as they all climbed into the car and drove towards the big house on the hill.

Chapter 2
The old chest in the attic

"You've got the same bedroom as last year, Amanda," said Aunty Rachel, as they all got out of the car outside the big house.

"The one next to mine," said Brenda. "We'll help you unpack[1]. Race you up the stairs."

Both the girls and Peter ran up the wide staircase and along the corridor to the large bedroom overlooking[2] the fields.

"Beat you," said Brenda who had got there first.

"Only because you weren't carrying this heavy suitcase," said Amanda, putting it down on the bed and looking around the room.

"A bedroom all to myself this year – I don't have to share[3] with Mum and Dad," she cried.

***

Brenda helped Amanda unpack the suitcase and rucksack. Amanda carefully put the presents on the bed.

---

1 *to unpack* – auspacken
2 *overlooking* – mit Blick auf
3 *to share* – teilen

"This packet is for you, Brenda" said Amanda, "and this is for you, Peter."

"Thanks," said Brenda and quickly unwrapped[4] it. "Ooh, a lovely scarf with lots of animals on it," she cried.

"And I've got a Swiss army knife," said Peter.

"Well, you must write and thank Uncle and Aunty," said Aunty Rachel as she came into the room.

"And this is for you and this is for Uncle," said Amanda and gave her the last of the presents.

"I'll ring your mother and tell her you have arrived safely at Glenchurch Grange, and thank her for the presents at the same time; but now come and have some supper."

As Aunty started to leave the room she said: "Oh, what a lovely green feather there on the floor. Is that for me, too?"

Peter picked it up: "Where did that come from, Amanda?"

"I'll tell you at supper," said Amanda and they all went down where Uncle Bob was waiting in the dining room.

***

During the meal, Amanda described the strange boy, who called himself Arthur, and explained how she had found the green feather.

---

4 *to unwrap* – auswickeln

Brenda said: "I thought I saw someone dressed like that at the station, after we got into the car. For some reason, when I saw him, I suddenly remembered the old oak tree in the forest and the stories you told. But I don't think I've seen him before."

"That's funny," said Amanda, "he spoke to me about the old oak tree, too. And about the stories I told. But we never saw him last year, did we?"

"Well," said Uncle Bob, "I expect[5] he's from somewhere in the village and remembered you from last year." He laughed: "Most of the village children are in my school and, as I'm the headmaster[6], I'm supposed to know them all."

"Well," said Aunty Rachel, "it certainly is a beautiful feather. You must give it back to him, Amanda, if you see him in the village."

"If everyone has finished supper, let's go up to the old attic[7] room," said Brenda, "we're only allowed up there when you are here, Amanda."

"Only after you've done the washing up," said Aunty Rachel.

"Oh, groan, groan, groan[8]," said Brenda. "OK, come on, Amanda, and you too, Peter. I'll wash up and you two do the wiping."

---

5 *to expect* – annehmen
6 *headmaster* – Schulleiter
7 *attic* – Speicher
8 *groan* – seufz

It only took[9] them a few minutes to do the washing up and then they rushed up the two flights[10] of narrow stairs to the attic room. It was a large room at the top of the house and filled with marvellous things. There was an old rocking horse, an old doll's house with tiny furniture in it, and lots of old cupboards filled with cups and plates. And, most interesting of all, there were large wooden chests[11] mostly filled with old clothes. Last year they had found a key to one of the chests and opened it. It had been filled with old dresses and suits, and they had dressed up in the clothes.

Then Peter had found, in another corner, an old wind-up gramophone. So they had danced around the attic to the music of the old records they had found inside it.

9 *it takes them* – sie brauchen
10 *a flight of stairs* – Treppe
11 *chest* – Truhe

"I know," said Amanda, "let's open one of the other chests."

"Which one?" asked Brenda.

"Oh, you choose, Peter," answered Amanda.

"Eeny, meeny, miny, mo," said Peter. "This one." He pointed to an old chest under the window. It was covered in an old sheet[12]. They took the sheet off and looked at it.

"How old do you think this is?" asked Amanda.

"Oh, probably hundreds and hundreds of years old," answered Brenda. "Come on, let's open it and see what's inside."

There was a big leather handle[13] on the top, but it didn't matter how much they pulled, it just wouldn't open.

"It must be locked[14]," said Peter.

They all sat down on an old sofa and Brenda said: "Let's try to guess what's inside it."

"Old knives and forks," said Amanda.

"No, they're in the drawer[15] of that old cupboard." said Peter.

"I think it's full of hats," said Brenda.

Hats! Suddenly they both looked at each other.

"Are you thinking the same as me?" said Brenda.

"Could be," replied Amanda. "Were you thinking of that boy's hat and the green feather, too?"

---

12 *sheet* – Betttuch
13 *handle* – Griff
14 *to lock* – zusperren
15 *drawer* – Schublade

Brenda went very quiet: “Yes, I was.”

She went to the old chest and thoughtfully ran her fingers down one side.

“Here, look Amanda,” she cried, “feel this pattern[16].”

Peter pulled the chest into the room so that they could see it better. And there, roughly carved[17] on the side of the chest, was a long feather.

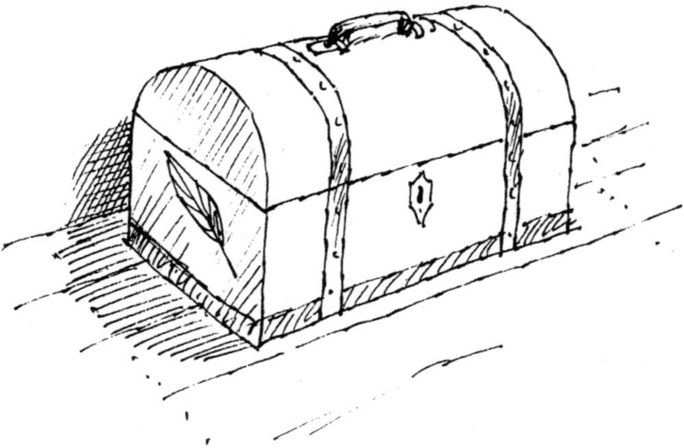

“Time for bed children,” called Aunty Rachel from the bottom of the stairs. “Up early tomorrow. We’re driving into Woodham for market day.”

---

16 pattern – Muster
17 *to carve* – schnitzen

Chapter 3
Market day in Woodham

"Woof, woof, woof," barked Susie excitedly. She ran round and round the car, as Uncle Bob carefully put the shopping baskets into the boot. Susie loved going to the market, too.

"OK," said Uncle Bob, "everyone in the car. Peter and you girls in the back seat and don't forget to fasten your seat belts." Susie sat on the floor, between their legs, panting[1] with excitement.

When they were driving along, Aunty Rachel asked: "What did you find in the attic, Brenda? Anything interesting? There are such a lot of things there. My old Uncle Damian had the house before us. He told me that some of them were very, very old."

"We tried the old chest under the window," said Peter, "but it was locked. Do you know if there is a key for it, Dad?"

"I know the chest you mean," said Uncle Bob. "Yes, that looks hundreds of years old. There must be a key for it somewhere. I'll look in my desk when we get home. Well, here we are at the market. Be careful that Susie doesn't run into the road when you get out."

---

1 *to pant* – nach Luft schnappen

***

It was a beautiful summer's morning as they arrived in Woodham. It was still quite early and some of the market people were just putting up their stalls.

"Now, children," said Uncle Bob, "you don't want to come shopping with us. Why don't you go off on your own? We'll meet for lunch at 12 o'clock at the Bell pub. You know, Peter, the one with the children's room at the back. Have you got any pocket money, Amanda?"

"Oh, yes," said Amanda, "Dad gave me twenty pounds to spend."

"Well don't spend it all at once," laughed Aunt Rachel, "and Peter, don't forget to look after Susie."

"Where shall we go first?" asked Amanda.

"Let's look at all the earring and necklace stalls[2]," replied Brenda. Last April, Brenda had had her ears pierced for her birthday.

"While you girls are trying on earrings, I'm going to the fishing tackle shop[3] for some new hooks[4]," said Peter who had had a fishing rod for his birthday present. "I'll take Susie with me."

---

2 *necklace stall* – Halskettenstand

3 *fishing tackle shop* – Geschäft für Fischereibedarf

4 *hook* – Haken

Amanda and Brenda went from one stall to another looking at all the jewellery. Brenda enjoyed herself trying on all the different shaped earrings and looking at herself in the mirrors hanging on the stalls. Amanda didn't have pierced ears, but she was trying on the necklaces. She loved the coloured stones on the long chains.

***

It was about ten o'clock when they had looked at all the jewellery stalls and it was starting to get quite warm.

"Oh, look," said Brenda, "there's an ice cream van over there. Let's have an ice cream."

"Good idea," said Amanda and then they had to decide on which flavour[5] to buy.

"I'll have vanilla," said Amanda. Brenda finally chose a strawberry one.

Suddenly, there was a little "woof" and Susie was looking up at them hopefully. Peter was just behind her.

"And a chocolate one for Susie," Amanda told the ice cream seller.

"I thought I would find you here," said Peter as he ordered an ice cream, too.

"Let's go and sit on that seat over there," said Brenda.

They all sat down on the seat in the town square. Amanda unwrapped Susie's ice cream and put it on the ground. Susie enjoyed licking it off the wrapper[6]. While they were eating their ices, they watched the stalls. They were getting busier and busier. People were trying on clothes here and hats there. Some were buying vegetables and fruit, others were buying ham or cheese.

***

Suddenly, between the people buying food, Amanda saw the strangely dressed boy standing at a stall.

"Look, Brenda, I think that is the boy Arthur over there," she said. "Can you see him?"

---

5 *flavour* – Geschmack
6 *wrapper* – Umhüllung

"Where?" asked Brenda who was still licking her strawberry ice cream.

"By that leather bag stall next to the jewellery one," replied Amanda. "Let's go and talk to him."

"Let's finish our ices first," said Peter. "You watch where he goes."

By the time they had finished their ices, Amanda couldn't see him in the crowd.

"You imagined[7] it," said Brenda. "Like one of your stories."

"No, I didn't," said Amanda. "Look, there he is, near that fruit stall. Quick, let's run after him."

They ran between the shoppers with Susie running behind, but there were so many people that they could not catch up with him. When they got to the last place Amanda had seen him, they were out of breath.

"Phew," said Peter, "he's certainly hard to find, isn't he?"

"I think he went between that secondhand book stall and the one selling antique silver and things," said Amanda.

When they arrived, Susie ran in front and went between the two stalls. She gave a little bark and they started to follow her. Suddenly they all stopped and there, in front of them, a long green feather was slowly floating[8] to the ground.

---

7 *to imagine* – sich einbilden
8 *to float* – schweben, treiben

Chapter 4
A pub lunch

After Uncle Bob and Aunt Rachel had done most of their shopping, Aunt Rachel said: "Let's go for a coffee before the café is too crowded[1]."

"Why not," said Uncle Bob.

They went to their favourite coffee shop, sat at a table, and ordered their coffee.

When it arrived, Aunt Rachel said: "I wonder[2] what those children are up to[3]."

"Eating ice cream if I know them," laughed Uncle Bob. "I wonder if they have seen that strange village boy. What was his name? Arthur, wasn't it?"

"You would know him if he was in your school, Bob," said Aunt Rachel.

"Yes, I suppose so," replied Uncle Bob thoughtfully[4]. "It's strange, but I have a feeling I know a story of someone called Arthur. Just like Amanda described him. A boy in old clothes."

"If it wasn't for that green feather," said Aunt Rachel, "I would have said she fell asleep on the train and dreamed it."

---

1 *crowded* – voll von Menschen
2 *I wonder* – mich würde interessieren
3 *to be up to* – machen
4 *thoughtfully* – nachdenklich

"Yes," said Uncle Bob, "but that feather reminds me of something, too. I'll remember it later I expect[5]."

"Oh, never mind," said Aunt Rachel, "let's finish our shopping then walk down to the pub to meet the children."

***

Amanda, Brenda, Peter and Susie were still looking for the strange boy among the busy market stalls.

Then Brenda said, "Oh, goodness, look at the time, it's ten past twelve. Mum and Dad will think we are lost. Come on Amanda, we won't find Arthur in this crowd. It's quite a long way to the Bell."

They walked quickly back through the market to the town square and Peter led the way down a side street to the pub. They went into the children's room at the back[6]. Uncle Bob and Aunt Rachel were already sitting at a table.

---

5 *to expect* – erwarten
6 *at the back* – hinten

"You're late," said Uncle Bob, "we were getting worried."

"Never mind," said Aunt Rachel, "you are here now. Let's look at the menu[7]."

"Shepherd's pie for me," said Brenda.

"Sausage and mash potatoes[8] for me," said Peter.

"And I'll have fish and chips. Lots of chips. With tomato ketchup!" said Amanda.

***

While they were waiting for the food to arrive, Amanda said: "Look what we found." She laid the long green feather on the table. "We saw that boy Arthur in the market, but he disappeared[9] before we could reach[10] him. And then we found this."

Uncle Bob picked it up thoughtfully.

"Someone told me a story once about a boy like you describe," he said, "but it was a long, long time ago. It can't be the same boy."

"Oh, tell us the story while we're waiting for our food," said Brenda.

"Yes, please," said Amanda.

"I can't remember it exactly," replied Uncle Bob, "but I think it was about a boy living in the woods with his grandmother. He was a clever boy, but she wouldn't let

---

7 *menu* – Speisekarte
8 *mash potatoes* – Kartoffelbrei
9 *to disappear* – verschwinden
10 *reach* – erreichen

him go to school. I'll try to find out more about the story, if you like."

"Ah, here's our lunch now, children," said Aunty Rachel. "Not too much tomato ketchup, Amanda, or it'll come out of your ears!"

Chapter 5
A picnic and a visit to Blackie

"It's a lovely morning," said Brenda, the next day. She bounced[1] up and down on the bed that Amanda was sleeping on.

"Come on, lazy bones. Let's have breakfast and go down to look at the horses and then look for blackberries[2] in the woods."

"OK," said Amanda, "if you'll stop bouncing on the bed I'll get up."

"I'll show you Blackie first and then we can go to the oak tree and you can tell me some more stories. Like we did last year," continued Brenda. Blackie belonged to Farmer Redmond. He had a riding school and was teaching Brenda to ride.

Peter called out: "I'll come with you as far as the old bridge. I'm going fishing. I saw some trout[3] in the stream there last week."

***

At breakfast, Uncle Bob said: "I've looked in all the

---

1 *to bounce* – springen
2 *blackberry* – Brombeere
3 *some trout* – einige Forellen

usual[4] places, Peter, but I can't find the key to that chest in the attic."

"You'll probably find it when you're looking for something else," laughed Aunty Rachel. "What are you children going to do on this lovely morning?"

"We're going to see Blackie and then go looking for blackberries in the woods," said Brenda and Amanda together.

"And I'm going to the river fishing," said Peter. "Last week I saw some trout near the old bridge."

"Well, I'll make you some sandwiches and there are some tins of coke in the fridge," said Aunty Rachel.

"Put in some apples for Blackie, too," called out Brenda.

"Watch out for Merlin," said Uncle Bob. "You know, the magician[5] of King Arthur. He'll change you girls into frogs."

"Dad's only joking," said Brenda, "Merlin is what we call the old badger[6] who comes snuffling around for titbits[7] some evenings."

"Don't get lost in the woods," said Aunty Rachel, as she gave them their picnic basket and waved them goodbye, "and don't fall in the river, Peter."

"And don't forget to shut all the farm gates," Uncle Bob called out as the children ran along the path, with Susie barking at their heels[8].

---

4 *usual* – üblich
5 *magician* – Zauberer
6 *badger* – Dachs
7 *titbit* – Leckerbissen
8 *heel* – Ferse

***

The first gate they came to led into a field with lots of sheep with their lambs.

"Come here, Susie," said Brenda and picked up the wriggling[9] dog.

"Farmer Redmond lets us cross this field. It's a short cut[10] to the horses, but he doesn't like dogs chasing his lambs," explained Brenda.

When they reached the other side of the field, they carefully closed the gate behind them. Brenda put Susie down and she was off like a rocket. She was soon sniffing in all the holes she could find. Suddenly she found a rabbit and chased it for a few metres but it soon went into its hole.

"I hope it scratches your nose," said Peter. Peter had a pet rabbit at home, called Billy.

Then they came to the river and followed it across the meadows[11] and into the woods. When they came to the little bridge, Peter said good-bye to them.

"I hope you catch some nice fish," said Amanda, as Peter went along the river bank with his rod[12] and flies.

"If you do we can have them for supper," called out Brenda.

---

9 *to wriggle* – zappeln
10 *short cut* – Abkürzung
11 *meadow* – Wiese
12 *rod* – Angel (für Fische)

The two girls followed the path towards the field with the horses. Susie started snuffling in a big hole under a tree.

"What's she after?" asked Amanda.

"Leave that hole alone, Susie," said Brenda, "that's the home of old Merlin our pet badger. Dad says a badger's hole is called a set."

At last they came to the field with the horses and Amanda opened the gate. Brenda called and Blackie heard her and came galloping over.

"You can give him an apple, too, Amanda," said Brenda rubbing Blackie's nose.

Soon the apples were gone and Blackie gave a whinney[13] and galloped back to the other horses. Brenda gave him a last wave and closed the gate behind them.

13 *whinney* – Wiehern

They went along the path again until they came to the wood.

There they started looking for blackberries.

"It's a bit early for them yet," said Brenda when they had only found one or two. "We'll look again before the end of the holidays."

Then they walked on through the wood and soon came to a big open area. In the middle, the big old oak tree was still there. Susie ran to the tree and started barking.

"What's she barking at?" asked Amanda.

"I don't know," answered Brenda, "perhaps at those big black birds at the top."

They looked up and several rooks[14] flew away. They were cawing[15] angrily at Susie for disturbing their peace.

"Let's have our lunch now," suggested[16] Brenda. "I'm quite hungry after giving all those apples to Blackie. Let's see what Mum has given us."

***

They sat down under the tree and opened the picnic basket. Susie gave a "woof" and sat in front of them. Her bright eyes were shining and her was tail wagging.

---

14 *rook* – Krähe
15 *to caw* – krächzen
16 *to suggest* – vorschlagen

“She is saying ‘What have you got for me?’” Amanda said.

“It’s okay, Susie,” said Brenda, “Mum has put in a nice ham bone for you to chew.” Susie took it in her mouth and ran behind the tree to eat it.

After they had eaten their sandwiches and drunk their cola, they lay back and looked up through the oak’s branches at the blue sky above them.

“Tell me another nice story, Amanda,” said Brenda.

“What about?” said Amanda.

“I know, tell a story with that boy Arthur in it.”

Amanda lay back on the warm grass, closed her eyes, and started to think.

“Well, once upon a time,” Amanda began, “there was a cottage[17] near this oak tree. The tree then was part of a very big forest. In the cottage lived a boy and his old grandmother. They collected wood in the forest and sold it to the people in the village. They used it for their fires in the winter.”

“Sounds a bit like the story Dad started to tell us in the pub,” interrupted Brenda. “Shsh,” said Amanda. “It’s my story.”

“Anyway,” Amanda continued, “the old grandmother was very hard on the boy. She often shouted at him when he didn’t bring enough wood out of the forest. Once[18], when the boy was ten years old, the old priest from the village came to the cottage.

---

17 *cottage* – Hütte
18 *once* – einmal

'I'll give Arthur some lessons,' he said, 'in exchange for some fire wood for my church house.' Grandmother didn't like it, but agreed in the end. The priest soon found that Arthur learnt very quickly. Later, the priest told the grandmother that the boy was clever and should go to the village school."

"I hate school," said Brenda.

"Me too," said Amanda, "especially writing essays, but stop interrupting me, Brenda. Grandmother then said: 'And who is going to collect the villagers' wood? I'm much too old now. I looked after him when his parents died. Now he can look after me.'"

"She sounds a horrible old witch[19]," interrupted Brenda again.

"Shhh," said Amanda, "before he left, the old priest gave the boy something to write with.

'Practise doing your lessons when you can, Arthur,' he said kindly.

When the old priest had left, the boy's grandmother shouted at the boy: 'Never mind those silly ideas. Get out into the forest and collect plenty of wood or you'll get no supper tonight.'

The boy sadly put the writing things into the chest under his bed and went out into the forest.

'And stop carving things on the pieces of wood before you bring them home,' she shouted after him.

"Poor boy," said Brenda. "I wouldn't like Mum to stop my hobby, riding Blackie. Is that all, Amanda?"

---

19 *witch* – Hexe

Amanda closed her eyes and thought for a few minutes. "No," she said, "when Arthur had gone out for more wood, his grandmother locked Arthur's chest with a big iron key.[20] Then she hid the key in a small wooden box and locked it in a cupboard."

***

It was very hot now and there was a long, long pause as Brenda and Amanda lay day-dreaming in the afternoon sun. Brenda was thinking about Blackie and Amanda about the wooden chest in the old cottage.

Suddenly Susie was barking: "Woof, woof, woof," and Brenda sat up quickly with a start.

"My goodness, it's five o'clock," she said. "We must have fallen asleep."

Susie was dancing excitedly[21] around the oak tree and trying to jump up the trunk.

"What's she barking at?" asked Amanda.

"Oh, it's probably those black birds in the tree again," replied Brenda.

---

20 *iron key* – eiserner Schlüssel
21 *excited* – aufgeregt

They both looked up through the branches to see what Susie was barking at. Then they both saw it at the same time: a long green feather was resting[22] on a branch, just above their heads.

22 *to rest* – ruhen

Chapter 6
The story of the charcoal burners

Aunt Rachel was sitting in the kitchen when Uncle Bob came in.

"I've just been down to the library," said Uncle Bob, "I was interested in that strange boy Amanda saw. In the library, there are some old books about local history. I borrowed[1] this one, and in it is a story about the old charcoal burners[2] who lived in the forest that was around the village. That was many years ago and most of the forest has gone now. That big old oak tree in the open area must be one of the last from the old forest."

"I've been trying to remember something, too," said Aunty Rachel. "My old Uncle Damian used to collect antiques. When I was a girl, I sometimes went with him.

I remember going to old houses and cottages when they were sold. He often bought chests and old

1 *to borrow* – sich ausleihen
2 *charcoal burner* – Köhler

furniture. After he died, they were stored up in the attic room. They were still there when we moved into the house. And that was many years ago."

"That's funny," said Uncle Bob, "in the old book there was a story about an old charcoal burner's cottage. It said it was quite near that old oak tree. Perhaps Uncle Damian bought things there before it was knocked down."

"What else did you find out?" asked Aunty Rachel.

"Well, not much," said Uncle Bob, "but after I left the library I went to the pub. Old Bill, the gardener was in there and he saw the book. I told him about Amanda's mysterious[3] boy Arthur. He said he remembered hearing about a story of a boy who lived in the forest, long, long ago."

"The story he heard was that a young boy delivered[4] firewood to the people in the village. When he was in the village, the children liked to listen to him, because he told them marvellous[5] stories. The children also knew he couldn't stay very long, because his grandmother treated[6] him very badly.

He also heard stories that, even now, some village children say they sometimes see a strange boy, either[7] in the village or sometimes in the woods."

"Funny," said Aunt Rachel, "but I know old Bill, he likes telling a good story when he's in the pub, too."

---

3 *mysterious* – geheimnisvoll
4 *to deliver* – liefern
5 *marvellous* – wundersam
6 *to treat* – behandeln
7 *either ... or* – entweder ... oder

Just then there was a noise outside.

"Hello," said Aunty Rachel, "I can hear Susie barking. That must be the girls."

***

"Hello Mum, we're back," said Brenda excitedly. "After we gave Blackie the apples, we went through the woods to the old oak tree. Show them, Amanda, show them what we found."

Amanda put the new green feather carefully on the table. "My goodness, Amanda," said Uncle Bob, "you're collecting lots of them, aren't you?"

Then Brenda told them about the story Amanda had told, while they were under the old oak tree.

"There was a big wooden chest in the story. I think she was thinking about the one in the attic," said Brenda.

"Well, I think it's about time I took a look at this old chest," said Uncle Bob. "Come on. Let's go and have a look."

Uncle Bob led[8] the way up into the attic. "I haven't been up here for years and years," he said. "Now where's this wonderful chest of yours?"

Amanda showed Uncle Bob the chest under the window.

---

8 *lead, led, led* – führen

"Hm," he said, "it's certainly very, very old. I don't think we have got a key, anywhere, that would fit[9] this old lock."

"Tell Dad about your story of the small wooden box that was in the cottage," said Brenda.

"Yes," she said, "I imagined there was a small wooden box in the old cottage in the forest and the key for the chest was hidden in it. The box had a round top with metal bands round it."

"Well, let's have a good look around the attic," suggested Aunty Rachel, "perhaps Uncle Damian bought a box like that, too."

They searched every corner of the attic and found many old boxes, but none of them had a round top or metal bands. Also none of them had any keys in them.

"Never mind[10]," said Aunty Rachel, "I expect we'll find it one day."

***

Suddenly there was a shout from downstairs. "That's Peter come home. Let's go down and see if he caught any trout. I expect you are all hungry now after all this excitement."

Disappointed, Amanda and Brenda followed Uncle Bob and Aunty Rachel down the stairs.

Peter was smiling when they got to the kitchen.

---

9 *to fit* – passen
10 *never mind* – das macht nichts

"I caught three trout," said Peter, "look." Three silver trout lay in his fishing bag.

"One each for your supper, children," said Uncle Bob.

Amanda and Brenda laid the table while Aunty Rachel cooked the meal.

Half way through supper, Amanda suddenly said: "Do you know, when I imagined that small box in my story, I had a feeling that I have seen it somewhere recently[11]."

"Perhaps you have a similar box in your house," said Uncle Bob.

"No," said Amanda, "I've seen it while I've been here with you."

"Well," said Brenda, "we've only been playing around the house or in the woods."

"We've been to the market in Woodham, too," said Peter.

"That's it," said Amanda, "I must have seen it at the market. Perhaps on one of the stalls when we looked at the jewellery."

"Well, we are going again next Saturday. You can have a look for it then," said Aunty Rachel. "Now help me wash up and then you can watch some television before going to bed."

---

11 *recently* – kürzlich

Chapter 7
The wooden box

Brenda and Amanda spent the next few days looking around the village, but they didn't see anybody like the boy Arthur. They even went back to the old oak tree a couple of times[1], after giving Blackie some more apples again.

"Only one more day to wait," said Brenda, "and then we're off to Woodham market again. I can try on some more earrings while you are searching the stalls for that old box."

At last it was Saturday and again Susie was barking in her excitement, but this time Amanda was more excited even than Susie.

"This week we'll meet at Kay's coffee shop at half-past-ten and you can tell us if you've had any success[2]," said Uncle Bob as they got out of the car.

While Aunty Rachel and Uncle Bob were shopping, the two children started looking along the stalls. Brenda was more interested in trying on earrings again. Peter, of course, went straight[3] to the fishing tackle shop.

"I need some more flies and hooks," he said. "I'll see you at the coffee shop."

---

1 *a couple of times* – ein paarmal
2 *success* – Erfolg
3 *straight* – direkt

"Oh, come on," said Amanda after the third stall, "you tried those earrings on last week."

***

After they had been about half an hour searching among the secondhand and antique stalls, Amanda suddenly stopped quite still.

"What is it?" asked Brenda.

"Look," said Amanda pointing[4] to the antique stall.

There at the back of the stall, among lots of old wooden carvings and silverware, was a small wooden box with metal bands.

"Look," she whispered again, "there it is, I'm sure of it."

---

4 *to point to* – zeigen auf

"You could be right," said Brenda, "and look, this is exactly where we found the green feather. Right next to this stall."

"Can I help you, young ladies?" said the stall holder.

"Yes, please. How much is that box?" asked Amanda, pointing to it. Her finger was trembling[5].

"Oh, that old thing," said the stall holder, "you can have that for ten pounds, my dear." He handed the box to her and when she shook it, something rattled[6] inside. She opened it and a large old iron key fell out.

"And for an extra pound you can have the key as well," laughed the stall holder.

Amanda looked in her purse. Yes, she still had fifteen pounds left.

"OK," she said, "here's the eleven pounds." The stall holder took the money and said: "Shall I wrap it for you?"

"No, that's okay," replied Amanda

"You'll be able to keep all your jewellery in it," said the stall holder, still laughing.

"Come on," said Brenda, "lets go and show Mum and Dad."

***

When they got to the coffee shop Uncle Bob and Aunty Rachel were not there, so the children ordered a coke

---

5 *to tremble* – zittern
6 *to rattle* – klappern

each and waited patiently[7].

"So, you found something," said Uncle Bob as he and Aunty Rachel came in and sat down at the table.

He looked at the box and then at the key and said: "I think you have been lucky, Amanda. I think this key will fit the old chest. We'll try it this afternoon."

Amanda couldn't wait for the shopping to be finished. They went to the pub for lunch, again.

"Hey, go easy[8] with the tomato ketchup," laughed Uncle Bob, as Amanda quickly ate her meal, "there's more ketchup than chips."

When they got back home at last, they all went up to the attic. Amanda took the key from the box and put it in the lock.

She tried to turn it but it wouldn't move.

"Let me try," said Uncle Bob. But, he too, could not turn[9] it. "The lock is probably very rusty[10]," he said. "Peter, get some of your bike oil." Peter quickly fetched the oil and Uncle Bob put some in the lock and on the key.

"Snap." Ten minutes later the lock clicked back.

"Right, Amanda" said Uncle Bob, "you must be the first to open the box."

***

---

7 *patient* – geduldig
8 *to go easy* – sei sparsam
9 *to turn* – drehen
10 *rusty* – rostig

Creak, creak, went the old hinges[11] as Amanda pushed the heavy lid[12] up. Then she looked down inside.

11 *hinge* – Türangel
12 *lid* – Deckel

Chapter 8
The last green feather

So now the holidays were over. They all had to start school again next week.

"Groan, groan," Brenda said as Uncle Bob, Aunty Rachel and Peter waved goodbye. Susie was barking, as usual, up at the train window.

Before long the train was arriving back in Basington Station. Amanda's mother and father were waiting for her. They were pleased to see her back and even brother Sam said she looked quite brown from the country holiday.

"Fatter though," he said in his usual brotherly way and asked: "What have you got in that old box?"

"Oh, not much," replied Amanda. "I bought it at Woodham Market."

***

She didn't tell him about her disappointment when she had looked down into the old chest.

"There's nothing in it," she had said.

Then Uncle Bob, Aunty Rachel, Brenda and Peter all looked inside, too.

"That's not true, Amanda," said Aunty Rachel, "Look, there is some old paper with some writing on it."

"Yes, and here is what is left of some old feathers," said Uncle Bob.

They had taken out the scraps[1] and looked at the bits and pieces carefully.

"Poor Amanda. You were expecting a treasure[2], weren't you?" said Aunty Rachel.

"I was," said Brenda. "Lots of earrings and necklaces."

"Look," said Uncle Bob. He had been looking closely at the things from the chest. "These are not just[3] feathers, they are old quill pens[4]." He showed Amanda the carefully shaped[5] end of the old feathers.

"Well," said Aunty Rachel, "it's certainly similar[6] to the story you told us. Do you think the boy you met on the train was the Arthur in your story? Perhaps this is his writing on this paper."

"Now Amanda, you have collected three green feathers," said Uncle Bob, "If you give them to me I'll make you three children a copy of this quill pen. Then you'll at least have a souvenir of this year's visit."

Three days later Amanda was back at school.

"And for your homework today, children, I want you

---

1 *scrap* – Fetzen
2 *treasure* – Schatz
3 *not just* – nicht bloß
4 *quill pen* – Federkiel
5 *shaped* – geformt
6 *similar* – ähnlich

to write a story about your holidays," said Mrs Hemming, Amanda's teacher. Amanda groaned. She could tell nice stories but writing essays was her worst subject.

That evening Amanda sat down to do her homework. She sat there for a long time, but didn't know how to start. Then she looked at the old box. She hadn't shown Sam or her parents the beautiful long green quill pen that Uncle Bob had made. He had given her some ink to use with the pen, too.

She opened the box and took out the lovely long green feather. She turned it over and watched the colours go from green to gold. She put it down and slowly opened the ink bottle. She dipped the quill into it, then she opened her school book.

***

Suddenly, she remembered all the stories from under the oak tree. She started to write. The pen started to move easily over the paper: "Once upon a time[7] there was a young boy called Arthur. He lived with his old grandmother in a cottage in a big forest. His grandmother made him collect fire wood to sell to the people in the village –."

At that moment, Amanda thought she heard a happy laugh. She looked up from her school book. Perhaps it was her brother Sam coming to ask questions about his

---

7 *once upon a time* – es war einmal

homework. She looked towards the door, but no one was in the room. Then, as she started to write again, she saw it. A beautiful, long, green feather was lying on top of the old wooden box.

(Bitte blättern Sie um)

Französisch

Landeskunde Frankreich	Best.-Nr. 94501
Wortschatz	Best.-Nr. 94503
Literatur	Best.-Nr. 94502
Abitur-Wissen Literaturgeschichte	Best.-Nr. 94506
Kompakt-Wissen Abitur Themenwortschatz	Best.-Nr. 945010
Lektüre Renée Hazard: *La Cité des Roses et autres contes et nouvelles*	Best.-Nr. 255001

Latein

Abitur-Wissen Lateinische Literaturgeschichte	Best.-Nr. 94602
Kurzgrammatik	Best.-Nr. 94601
Wortkunde	Best.-Nr. 94603
Kompakt-Wissen Kurzgrammatik	Best.-Nr. 906011
Lektüre Seneca: *Epistulae morales ad Lucilium* – Buch 1	Best.-Nr.260001
Lektüre *Rom und die Christen*	Best.-Nr. 260003
Lektüre *Die Frau im antiken Rom*	Best.-Nr. 260005
Lektüre *Antike Medizin*	Best.-Nr. 260007
Lektüre *Petri Abaelardi Historia Calamitatum*	Best.-Nr. 260008

Deutsch

Training Methoden Deutsch	Best.-Nr. 944062
Deutsch 11. Klasse	Best.-Nr. 90405
Aufsatz Oberstufe	Best.-Nr. 84401
Abitur-Wissen Erörtern und Sachtexte analysieren	Best.-Nr. 944064
Abitur-Wissen Textinterpretation Lyrik, Drama, Epik	Best.-Nr. 944061
Abitur-Wissen Deutsche Literaturgeschichte	Best.-Nr. 94405
Abitur-Wissen Prüfungswissen Oberstufe	Best.-Nr. 94400
Kompakt-Wissen Rechtschreibung	Best.-Nr. 944065
Lexikon Autoren und Werke	Best.-Nr. 944081

Religion

Katholische Religion 1 – gk	Best.-Nr. 84991
Katholische Religion 2 – gk	Best.-Nr. 84992
Abitur-Wissen gk ev. Religion Der Mensch zwischen Gott und Welt	Best.-Nr. 94973
Abitur-Wissen gk ev. Religion Die Verantwortung des Christen in der Welt	Best.-Nr. 94974
Abitur-Wissen Glaube und Naturwissenschaft	Best.-Nr. 94977
Abitur-Wissen Jesus Christus	Best.-Nr. 94978
Abitur-Wissen Die Frage nach dem Menschen	Best.-Nr. 94990
Abitur-Wissen Die Bibel	Best.-Nr. 94992
Abitur-Wissen Christliche Ethik	Best.-Nr. 94993
Lexikon Ethik und Religion	Best.-Nr. 94959
Lektüre Heinz Zahrnt: *Stammt Gott vom Menschen ab?*	Best.-Nr. 297001

Ethik

Ethische Positionen in historischer Entwicklung – gk	Best.-Nr. 94951
Abitur-Wissen Philosophische Ethik	Best.-Nr. 94952
Abitur-Wissen Glück u. Sinnerfüllung	Best.-Nr. 94953
Abitur-Wissen Freiheit und Determination	Best.-Nr. 94954
Abitur-Wissen Recht und Gerechtigkeit	Best.-Nr. 94955
Abitur-Wissen Religion und Weltanschauungen	Best.-Nr. 94956
Abitur-Wissen Wissenschaft – Technik – Verantwortung	Best.-Nr. 94957
Abitur-Wissen Politische Ethik	Best.-Nr. 94958
Lexikon Ethik und Religion	Best.-Nr. 94959

Fächerübergreifend

Richtig Lernen Tipps u. Lernstrategien – Oberstufe	Best.-Nr. 10483
Referate u. Facharbeiten – Oberstufe	Best.-Nr. 10484
Methoden-Training – Meinungen äußern, Ergebnisse präsentieren	Best.-Nr. 10486

Natürlich führen wir noch mehr Titel für alle Schularten. Wir informieren Sie gerne!

Telefon: 0 81 61/179-0
Internet: www.stark-verlag.de
Telefax: 0 81 61/179-51
E-Mail: info@stark-verlag.de

Bestellungen bitte direkt an:

STARK Verlagsgesellschaft mbH & Co. KG
Postfach 1852 · 85318 Freising

STARK

14-V1T